LET'S GRILL!

Texas' Best Secret BBQ Recipes

David Martin

Disclaimer

Disclaimer and Terms of Use: Effort has been made to ensure that the information in this book is accurate and complete, however, the author and the publisher do not warrant the accuracy of the information, text and graphics contained within the book due to the rapidly changing nature of science, research, known and unknown facts and internet. The author and the publisher do not hold any responsibility for errors, omissions or contrary interpretation of the subject matter herein. This book is presented solely for motivational and informational purposes only.

Table of Contents

Table of Contents

What's a BBQ?

When you live in a place that enjoys many sunny days each year, you want to spend time outside whenever possible. For Texans, the weather might mean searing hot days, cool evenings, strong wind, ice storms, drought and torrential rains. No matter. We are trail blazers, we are innovators, and we are fearless. We love our state more than any other residents love theirs. Therefore, we are going to cook outside even under less-than-ideal conditions. When we want our BBQ ribs and chicken, grilled vegetables or smoked brisket, we are going to brave the elements to have it. Perfect sunny days with friends and family are just extra nice.

Texans are also very specific, and have very strong opinions, when it comes to cooking techniques and the apparatus used. Grilling is not the same as BBQ or smoking!

Grill – meaning cooking directly over high heat or fire quickly.

It's also a wire or metal apparatus suspended over the heat.

Barbecue – a slow method of cooking over indirect heat, which may impart a "smoke" taste into the food. Generally accompanied by a wet sauce.

It's also a wire or metal apparatus suspended over the heat, but will likely be part of an enclosed cavern.

Smoking – it's close to barbecue but is usually even lower heat for a longer period. The smoke permeates all the meat. There is concentrated flavor on the exposed outside edges and it's clearly evident when you look at the meat.

While there is a metal grid, or spit, supporting the meat, the enclosed cavern will have a door for adding wood, keeping the smoke contained and the low fire burning.

A well-seasoned cast iron skillet is essential in a Texas kitchen. They're used by cooks on cattle drives and by your grandmother. They are virtually indestructible. Just don't let them soak in water. Texas grandmothers will "git" after "y'all" for that.

So, are you ready to cook? Not so fast. Any of the above three methods require preparation. There are marinades, dry rubs, and wet rubs, often called "mops." They not only tenderize the meat, they begin the flavoring process. Texans differ from other parts of the country with the rubs they use and the type of wood. Each of these adds another unique, tasty layer to the overall flavor profile.

Many cooks think that barbecue sauce is the crowning jewel of the carefully prepared and cooked food. In Texas, there are plenty who argue against sauce, too. Is BBQ sauce a "cheat" for someone who didn't take the time to impart the flavor during the cooking process? Or maybe the amazing sauce is the reason to eat the food in the first place.

In the following pages you will see great samples for each of the BBQ (and the other) techniques, marinades, rubs and sauces. It's not a meal without side dishes. Our selections represent the traditional Texas favorites. While you're waiting for the main course, serve up some tasty appetizers. You can't rush barbecue. In Texas, there is always room for dessert, too. The final chapter is dedicated to special sweets that finish up the perfect Texas BBQ meal.

Pick your favorites, review the preparation and call some friends over.
You can check the weather if you really want to, but in Texas we're going to have a BBQ party, rain or shine.

Beef

Slow Smoked Brisket

This is one of the foremost foods of Texas. It's just one of the beef dishes that reflect Texas' long history in the cattle industry. This recipe is about the technique, which requires proper equipment and patience. It is well worth the extra effort.

Serves 8–12 and keeps well in refrigerator

Ingredients
1 brisket, approximately 8–12 pounds
6–8 cups of wood chips (mesquite or pecan is recommended), soaked in water
1 batch brisket dry rub, recipe follows

Sauce Ingredients
1 quart apple juice
1 cup cider vinegar
1 cup barbecue sauce
Combine all ingredients.

Directions
Trim the brisket to 1/4 inch of outer fat including the fat near the flat and cap. Sprinkle the brisket with the dry rub and massage into meat. Wrap the brisket in foil and let sit in refrigerator at least 5 hours. Overnight is acceptable.

Set up your smoker per manufacturer's instructions. Place wood chips in box and bring smoker up to temperature. Unwrap the meat and place fat side up in the smoker. Brush the sauce on the brisket every hour. The brisket will need about 3–4 hours until internal temperature reaches 165°F.

Remove the brisket from the smoker, brush with sauce and wrap tightly in foil. Continue cooking another 3–4 hours. Final temperature should reach 190°F. Carefully remove the brisket, retaining all the juices. Allow to rest about 30 minutes prior to slicing.

The meat should be thinly sliced across the grain for serving.

Brisket Dry Rub

The dry ingredients of this rub are for a "crust" for a slowly smoked brisket. They add the flavors that permeate the meat in the smoking process. It can be made ahead of time and stored in an airtight container.

This recipe will cover a 10–12 pound brisket.

Ingredients
4 tablespoons paprika
3 tablespoons garlic powder
3 tablespoons celery salt
3 tablespoons mustard powder
2 tablespoons salt
2 teaspoons cayenne pepper
2 tablespoons packed dark brown sugar
2 tablespoons ground cumin
2 tablespoons freshly ground black pepper
2 tablespoons pure chili powder
1 tablespoon dried oregano
1 tablespoon dried basil
1 tablespoon onion powder
1 tablespoon ground white pepper

Directions
Stir all ingredients together until well blended. Store in airtight container.

Stuffed Bacon Cheeseburgers

Texans are particular about the proper burger patty. Simply, grilled burgers taste best with ground chuck. Many try to use sirloin or round, but 80/20 chuck gives you maximum flavor and moistness in the grilled hamburger. This recipe has some of the "fixin's" on the inside. Pile your favorite toppings on after they come off the grill.

Serves 4 large hamburger eaters

Ingredients
2 pounds ground chuck 80/20
2 ounces of white cheddar cheese, sliced into 4 pieces
2 ounces of Pepper Jack cheese, sliced into 4 pieces
8 strips of bacon, cooked until lightly crisp
Black pepper
Garlic powder
Vegetable oil
4 hamburger buns
Condiments and toppings
Wax paper

Directions
Divide the chuck into 8 even portions. The secret is to form 8 very thin patties. Place the portions on wax paper and cover with additional wax paper. Use the bottom of a heavy skillet as the press. Press to about 1/4" thin. Sprinkle the patties with fresh ground black pepper and garlic powder to taste.

Assemble 2 strips of crumbled bacon and 1 piece of each cheese in the center of 4 patties. Be sure the ingredients do not overhang the edges. Place the other 4 patties on top. Re-cover with wax paper and gently press around the edges to seal. Brush patties with vegetable oil on both sides.

Cook patties on hot grill. Do not flip more than once. About 5–7 minutes on each side, medium–well done.

Barbecue Fajitas

Plan ahead to allow the beef to marinate for 2 hours. The meat will grill up to be full of flavor and tenderized.

Serves 6–8

Ingredients
2 1/2 pounds of skirt steak, about 2 or 3 pieces
1 cup bottled salsa
1/2 cup red onion, roughly chopped
1/2 cup fresh cilantro
1 jalapeno, sliced
1/4 cup tequila
1/4 cup fresh lime juice
1/4 cup ketchup
Pepper

Directions
Place the skirt steak pieces in a shallow baking dish. Meanwhile, combine remaining ingredients in the food processor and process until most of the chunks are removed. Pour over steak and let marinate at least 2 hours.

Prepare a hot grill (medium-high for gas, or when the coals turn white). Place the steaks over the fire, brush with any additional marinade, and cook for about 7 minutes. Flip and continue cooking about 5–7 minutes more. Transfer to cutting board, tent with foil, and let rest prior to slicing. Serve with tortillas, rice, beans and grilled vegetables.

Cowboy Rib-Eye

This is a true steak lover's favorite. It is a premium cut and one of the most expensive. Texans often splurge on this one for holidays and special occasions. Make sure the butcher has bone-in steaks, or ask him to cut them for you.

Serves 4

Ingredients
4 10 ounce rib-eye steaks, bone in, 1 inch thick
1/2 stick of butter, room temperature
6 tablespoons fresh cilantro, chopped
1 clove garlic
1/4 teaspoon chili powder
1 teaspoon salt
1/2 teaspoon pepper

Preparation
Preheat grill.

Prepare the cilantro butter by combining butter, cilantro, garlic, cumin, and chili powder in a food processor. Pulse until cilantro is finely chopped. Scrape butter from processor onto plastic wrap. Shape into a log and roll tightly. Refrigerate until firm, then slice into 4 pieces.

When grill is hot, salt and pepper the steaks. Cook 4–5 minutes each side for a medium-rare steak.

To finish, remove steaks from grill and place on dinner plates. Top hot steaks with cilantro butter slice and serve.

Beef Street Tacos

The recipe creates charred, tenderized meat that is well flavored and wrapped in warm corn tortillas. It's topped with fresh vegetables, and special cheese.

Serves 4–6

Ingredients
1 1/2 pound flank steak
1/4 cup soy sauce
3 tablespoons vinegar
1/4 cup olive oil
2 cloves garlic, minced
1 lime, juiced, and 2 limes, quartered
1/2 teaspoon salt
1/2 teaspoon white pepper
1/2 teaspoon black pepper
1/2 teaspoon dried oregano
1/2 teaspoon dried cumin
1/2 teaspoon paprika
1/2 teaspoon chili powder
16 corn tortillas
1 onion, chopped
1/2 cup chopped cilantro
1 avocado, cubed
2 jalapenos, seeded and chopped
1 cup cotija cheese (may substitute other white cheese such as Jack, if desired)

Directions

In a mixing bowl, combine all ingredients except flank steak. Mix.
Place the flank steak in a large dish and pour the mixture over the steak. Cover and let marinate at least 2 hours (up to 8 hours).

Preheat grill. To cook, place flank steak over a hot grill until well browned, about 5–6 minutes each side. Remove to cutting board and let rest. Then cut into bite-size pieces.

To serve, warm the tortillas slightly to soften. Assemble tacos with meat, chopped onion, chopped cilantro, jalapenos, avocado pieces and cotija cheese.

Texan Smoked Beef Ribs

Whole beef ribs are a bit hard to find, but you usually can order them from a good butcher shop. The butcher can trim them for you, removing some of the fat and the membrane. It will make for more tender ribs. You can also do this at home. A simple rub, a few hours in the smoker, a mop sauce to keep them moist and tender, a flavorful BBQ glazing sauce and voila, the perfect beef ribs!

Serves 4- 6

Ingredients
6-8 lbs. whole beef ribs, trimmed

Rub Ingredients
2 tablespoons paprika
3 tablespoons garlic powder
3 tablespoons onion powder
2 tablespoons kosher salt
2 tablespoons freshly ground black pepper

Mop sauce ingredients
¼ cup vegetable oil
1 cup beef broth, reduced sodium
1/2 cup apple cider vinegar
1 tablespoon dry mustard
1 cup beer
1 tablespoon hot sauce
1 tablespoon dried onion flakes

1/4 cup Worcestershire sauce

BBQ sauce ingredients
1/2 cup chopped onions
2 cloves garlic, minced
1 tablespoon Dijon mustard
1/2 cup ketchup
1/2 cup tomato sauce
1/4 cup Worcestershire
1/4 cup apple cider vinegar
1 tablespoon liquid smoke
1 cup freshly brewed black coffee
1 tablespoon chili peppers, minced
1 tablespoon chili powder
1/2 teaspoon salt
2 tablespoons packed brown sugar

Directions
Stir all ingredients from the dry rub together until well blended. Rub generously the beef ribs on both sides. Let rest for 30 minutes.

In the meantime, set up your smoker per manufacturer's instructions. Place wood chips in the smoker box. For this recipe, mesquite wood chips will bring out the beef natural smoky flavors. Bring smoker up to a temperature of 225ºF.

When the smoker is ready, put the beef ribs, meat side down on the middle rack of smoker with a pan below catching the cooking juices and drippings. Let it cook for 30 minutes until a nice crust appears on the meat. Turn the ribs over. Let if cook for 2 hours.

In the meanwhile, mix all the ingredients of the mop sauce into a medium-sized saucepan. Bring to a boil and let simmer until it reduces in half, about 20 minutes. Start brushing the ribs on the meaty side every 15 minutes with mop sauce for 2h00.

To prepare the BBQ sauce, put all the ingredients in a saucepan. On high heat, bring to a boil, then decrease heat and let simmer until it thickens, about 20 minutes. With an immersion blender, pureed the sauce. You can use a food processor or blender for this step.

After 2h30 of cooking, the ribs are ready for glazing with the BBQ sauce, brushing both sides, every 30 minutes for another hour or two, depending on the size of the ribs. They will be ready when the meat easily falls off the bone when pinched with the fingers.

Let the ribs rest for 15-20 minutes before slicing. Serve with grilled corns on the cub, coleslaw, potato salad or baked beans.

Texas Chili

In this part of the country, chili does <u>not</u>, by any proper Texans definition, have beans. Beans are a separate dish. Period. We often use the term Bowl of Red, due to its powerful coloring and flavor, provided from the chilies used. A cast iron pot with a lid may be set directly onto your grill.

Serves 4–6

Ingredients

2 1/2 pounds boneless chuck roast, trimmed and cut into 3/4 inch cubes
2 ounces dried whole chilies, use Ancho, Guajillo, de Arbol, or a combination
1 1/2 teaspoons ground cumin
2 teaspoon sea salt
2 teaspoon black pepper
1 teaspoon white pepper
5 tablespoons vegetable oil

3 cloves garlic
1/3 cup onion, chopped
2 cups beef stock
2 cups water
2 tablespoons flour
1–2 tablespoons brown sugar
2 tablespoons apple cider vinegar
Sour cream
Corn chips
4 ounces cheddar cheese, grated
1 lime, quartered

Directions
Toast the chilies over a flame or medium-high heat about 3–5 minutes, turning. Do not let them burn. Remove and place in a bowl with hot water. Soak about 30–40 minutes until soft. When softened, split the chilies to remove the seeds. Place in blender with cumin, salt, black pepper, white pepper and 1/4 cup of water. Puree until smooth and set aside.

Put 2 tablespoons of vegetable oil in cast iron pot and heat on medium-high until it begins to smoke. Add the beef in portions, browning 2–3 minutes on each side. Add more oil if necessary and finish cooking beef and set aside.

Reduce to medium heat and cook garlic and onion in 1 tablespoon of oil until translucent, about 3 minutes, in the pot. Stir in flour and mix well. Add stock and water and stir to deglaze pan. Add the chili mixture, beef, brown sugar and apple cider vinegar. Bring to a boil then reduce to low heat, 1 1/2 to 2 hours until meat is tender.

To serve, ladle a helping of chili into hearty bowl. Top with cheddar cheese, corn chips, sour cream and a lime wedge.

Pork

BBQ Pulled Pork

Slowly roasting the pork keeps the meat tender and it shreds easily. Placing it in the smoker adds another layer of flavor. The All-Purpose Cider BBQ Sauce complements the pork nicely.

Ingredients
1 5–7 pound pork shoulder or butt
3 tablespoons paprika
2 tablespoons garlic powder
2 tablespoons brown sugar
2 tablespoons mustard powder
2 tablespoons salt
Hamburger buns
3–4 cups of wood chips (mesquite or pecan is recommended), soaked in water

Directions
Mix the dry ingredients together until well blended. Rinse and dry the pork. Rub spice blend all over the pork. Marinate at least 1 hour but may be done overnight, in the refrigerator.

Prepare smoker per manufacturer's instructions; add wood chips. Smoker temperature should be 225ºF. Place pork in smoker, cooking about 5–7 hours until temperature reaches 160ºF.

(For a completely indoor version, preheat oven to 300ºF. Place the pork in a roasting pan that has been lined with aluminum foil. Cover and bake for 5–6 hours until the thermometer reaches 160ºF.)

NOTE: If you have refrigerated overnight, remove the pork so that it returns to room temperature prior to cooking.

Allow the pork to rest for a few minutes. Place pork on a large cutting board. Use two forks to pull the meat shreds from the roast.

To serve, place pork on a toasted bun and pour on All-Purpose Cider BBQ Sauce. (Recipe follows)

All-Purpose Cider BBQ Sauce

This is a tangy BBQ sauce. It's great on pork but could also be used on chicken. The recipe makes about 2 cups but consider doubling the recipe so you have some on hand.

Ingredients
1 1/2 cups apple cider vinegar
1/3 cup light brown sugar
3/4 cup ketchup
3/4 cup brown mustard
3 cloves garlic, finely minced
1/4 onion, finely minced
1 teaspoon sea salt
1 teaspoon black pepper
1 teaspoon cayenne pepper

Directions
Combine all ingredients into a saucepan. Stir over medium heat about 10 minutes until sugar dissolves and onion and garlic are softened. Remove from heat and store in a lidded container.

Honey Spice Baby Backs

Plan ahead to rub the ribs down the night before. This gives the ribs a fantastic flavor base for the sticky, spicy glaze finish. The meat will fall off the bone.

Serves 4–6

Ingredients
2 slabs (about two pounds each) of baby back ribs
4 tablespoons five-spice powder
1 teaspoon ground ginger
2 teaspoons dark brown sugar
1 1/2 teaspoons salt
1/2 teaspoon black pepper

1 bottle medium dark beer for the braise

The Glaze
1/2 cup honey
2 tablespoons ketchup
2 teaspoons soy sauce

Directions

Mix the rub ingredients in a mixing bowl until blended. Rub on both side of ribs; cover and allow to marinate overnight.

Pour the beer in a roasting pan. Place the ribs bone-side down in a roasting pan. Cover tightly and cook 1 1/2 hours in a 325ºF oven. Baste 2 or 3 times.

Light the grill prior to ribs finishing in oven. Mix together the glaze. When ribs are done, remove from oven and place on a baking sheet. Brush the ribs with the glaze. Finish ribs on the grill, about 7 minutes each side until glaze darkens in spots.

Country Style Pork Ribs

These ribs are all meat, no bones! They cook down as the fat renders out, keeping the meat tender. Once cooked, they can be finished on the grill or in the oven to char up the All-Purpose Cider BBQ Sauce.

Serves 4

Ingredients
8 country-style pork ribs
1 tablespoon garlic powder
1 tablespoon onion powder
2 teaspoons salt
2 teaspoons pepper
2 cups All-Purpose Cider BBQ Sauce

Directions
Rub ribs with garlic powder, onion powder, salt and pepper. Preheat oven to 325°F.

Place ribs in a baking dish, meat side up. Cover and bake for 2 hours. Remove ribs from oven and drain excess liquid.

To finish, brush ribs with All-Purpose Cider BBQ Sauce. Place back on the barbecue grill for 20–30 minutes on medium-low heat.

Grilled Beer Brats

No barbecue recipe book is complete without a mention of brats. There are many types to choose from, so select your favorite. Cooking them in beer before placing them on the grill insures they are completely cooked to the inside.

Serves 6

Ingredients
6 purchased bratwurst
1/2 onion, sliced thickly
2 cans or bottles of beer
1 teaspoon garlic powder
1 teaspoon mustard powder
Pepper to taste
Mustard

Directions
Preheat grill for medium-high heat.

Combine the beer, onions, garlic powder, mustard powder and pepper in a large pot and bring to boil. Reduce heat to medium and add the bratwurst. Cook bratwursts about 10 minutes. Remove the bratwursts and turn off the heat under the pot.
Grill the brats 5 or 10 minutes until charred. Spoon onion out of beer mixture and serve as a topping, along with mustard, on the finished brats.

Spiced-Up Barbecue Pork Tenderloins

The tenderloins are a lean, delicate cut. This Asian-inspired marinade becomes the cooking glaze as well. Serve with your favorite rice and sautéed vegetables.

Serves 4–6

Ingredients
2 pork tenderloins
1/4 cup canola oil
1/4 soy sauce
1 tablespoon sesame oil
2 tablespoons rice wine or dry sherry
3 cloves garlic, finely minced
2 teaspoons chili paste
1/2 teaspoon white pepper
1/4 teaspoon salt
1 tablespoon light brown sugar
1 teaspoon ground ginger
1/4 teaspoon ground cinnamon
1/8 teaspoon ground clove
1/4 teaspoon ground cayenne

Directions

Place tenderloins in an oven-proof dish. Combine all other ingredients in a mixing bowl, stirring until a paste forms. Pour over tenderloins, cover with plastic wrap and let marinate 1 hour in refrigerator.

Remove tenderloins from refrigerator. Preheat grill. Cook tenderloins 5 minutes then turn to cook each side 5 minutes for a total of about 20–22 minutes. Brush remaining marinade on halfway through cooking process. Remove from grill and cover with additional foil to rest. Slice before serving.

Chicken

Pan BBQ Chicken

This recipe pounds the chicken out to tenderize the meat. It also reduces the cooking time on the grill.

Serves 4

Ingredients
4 boneless chicken breasts
Salt
Pepper
2 tablespoons olive oil
1 cup peach barbecue sauce (recipe follows)
2 tablespoons honey
1 tablespoon apple cider vinegar
3 cloves garlic, minced
2 teaspoons chili powder
1 teaspoon dried oregano
1 teaspoon dried thyme
2 fresh rosemary springs
1/4 cup water

Directions

Pound out chicken breasts to 1/2 inch thickness. Rub half the olive oil, salt, and pepper on both sides of the chicken breasts. Combine remaining ingredients in mixing bowl and stir to blend.

Preheat grill to medium-high. Place a large cast iron pan on the grill. Pour other half of the olive oil in pan. Cook chicken 3 or 4 minutes on each side. Reduce to low heat and add remaining ingredients. Stir to deglaze pan and coat chicken. Cook in sauce an additional 5–7 minutes until chicken is cooked through.

Peach Barbecue Sauce

The peaches add sweetness and make the sauce a little lighter. This is best used on poultry or pork, but some meatier fish like salmon can stand up to it also. Fresh or frozen peaches can be used.

Makes about 2 cups

Ingredients
1 1/2 cups peaches that have been peeled and chopped. About 2–3 fresh
1/2 cup ketchup
1 teaspoon chili powder
2 cloves garlic, finely minced
1 teaspoon fresh ginger, grated
2 tablespoons lemon juice
1 teaspoon soy sauce
1/4 teaspoon cinnamon
Salt and freshly ground pepper

Directions
Combine all ingredients in a saucepan and bring to a boil. Cover and reduce heat to low and let simmer about 8–10 minutes. Remove from heat.

When cool, use a blender to puree until smooth. Store in lidded container.

Beer Can Chicken

It's funny-looking, but creates a moist, flavorful chicken. You just have to come up with a half-full can of beer!

Serves 4–6

Ingredients
1 whole chicken, about 4 pounds
2 tablespoons olive oil
1 opened, half-full can of beer, room temperature.
2 tablespoons fresh thyme
1 tablespoon fresh oregano
1 sprig of rosemary
1 lemon, halved and about 1 tablespoon of zest
Salt and freshly ground pepper

Directions
Set up the grill for indirect heat, adjusting racks or placing coals to the sides.
Clean chicken. Rub with the olive oil, thyme, oregano, lemon zest, salt and a generous grind of black pepper.

Put the rosemary sprig into the half can of beer. Squeeze the juice of the lemon into the can. Lower the chicken onto the can, leg-side down so that it stands upright on its own. Place on the grill away from direct heat. Cover the grill and do not open for at least an hour. After one hour, check every 15 minutes until the meat thermometer reads 160–165°F when inserted into thigh. (Juices will run clear when done.)

Carefully remove chicken from HOT can using a spatula and tongs. Let rest about 10 minutes.

NOTE: Place a rimmed cookie sheet under the chicken and can when removing to catch any splashes.

BBQ Chicken Quarters

The dark meat of the chicken is the moistest. It soaks up the marinade and is finished with the BBQ sauce. If you don't want to brave the rainy weather, you can still get a BBQ fix by converting this recipe to indoor cooking.

Serves 4

Ingredients
4 chicken legs with thighs attached
1 cup All-Purpose Chicken & Fish Marinade (recipe follows)
1/2 cup onion, chopped
1/2 cup ketchup
1 teaspoon chili powder
1/2 teaspoon ground mustard
1/3 cup honey
2 tablespoons Worcestershire sauce
Salt and freshly ground pepper

Directions

Rinse chicken. Rub salt and pepper into the chicken quarters. Pour All-Purpose Chicken & Fish Marinade on quarters. Marinate for about 3 hours in the refrigerator. Take quarters out of the refrigerator about 20 minutes before cooking.

Combine all remaining ingredients in a mixing bowl and stir until blended. Reserve.

Light grill to medium-high or until coals have started to turn white. Place on grill and cook for 12–15 minutes. Turn chicken over and baste with half of the BBQ sauce. Cook an additional 9–12 minutes. Remove from grill and baste with remaining sauce.

For indoor preparation, place chicken quarters in a deep baking pan and pour BBQ sauce over them, coating well. Place in 400°F oven and bake for about 50 minutes, basting occasionally.

All-Purpose Chicken & Fish Marinade

This is a classic marinade, perfect on chicken, fish or shellfish. Marinate chicken or fish for about 3 hours, and shellfish for about an hour.

Makes about 2 cups

Ingredients
1 lidded 16-ounce jar
1 cup high-quality extra virgin olive oil
4 cloves garlic, finely minced
3 shallots, finely minced
2 green onions, finely minced
3 lemons, juiced and zested
3 limes, juiced and zested
6 tablespoons Dijon mustard
1 tablespoon brown sugar
1 tablespoon fresh thyme, chopped
2 tablespoons fresh parsley, chopped

Directions
Combine all ingredients into lidded jar. Shake well until mixture thickens and is well blended.

Hint: this can be done in a food processor as well. Store marinade in sealed jar in refrigerator.

Whole Spit-Grilled Chicken

Slowly the chicken rotates while you baste occasionally with wet mop for chicken (recipe follows) to create a moist bird. The skin is crisp and flavorful.

Serves 4–6

Ingredients
1 chicken, about 4 pounds
1 carrot, cut in half
1 celery stalk, cut in half
1/4 of an onion
1 lemon, sliced
4 cloves garlic
1 teaspoon fresh thyme
1 teaspoon paprika
1/2 teaspoon cumin

1/4 teaspoon turmeric
1 tablespoon dried parsley
1/2 teaspoon salt
1/2 teaspoon black pepper
Olive oil

Directions
Rinse, clean and dry the chicken. Place the carrot, celery, onion, lemon slices and garlic in the cavity. Truss the chicken, insert spit and secure. Stir together thyme, cumin, paprika, turmeric, parsley, salt and pepper.
Rub chicken with olive oil; sprinkle with herb mixture and rub into skin.

Grill chicken on rotisserie about 1 1/2 hours at around 300°F. Brush with wet mop (recipe follows) every 30 minutes. Internal temperature of thickest part of the thigh should be 165°F.

Wet Mop for Chicken

Enjoy this all-purpose wet mop on poultry, pork or fish. It has a well-blended group of spices and herbs to enhance the lighter meats.

Makes about a quart (4 cups).

Ingredients
4 cups apple cider vinegar
1 lemon, juiced, retain lemon
1 lime, juiced, retain lime
1 teaspoon ground rosemary
1 teaspoon ground thyme
1/2 teaspoon ground sage
5 bay leaves
1 teaspoon ground red pepper
2 teaspoons sugar
1 teaspoon pepper
1 teaspoon salt

Directions
Combine all ingredients, including whole lemon and lime, in a saucepan. Cover and bring to a boil over medium heat. Remove from heat and stir in sugar. Allow to cool, then strain out lemon, lime and bay leaves.

Store in airtight container in refrigerator. Use as a basting mop while cooking.

Margarita Chicken Nachos

This is a great appetizer, but also hearty enough to be a main course depending on how much leftover chicken you have. Grill up some extra chicken when the grill is lit. Then use it with this spicy, fresh salsa.

Serves 4–6 as an appetizer

Ingredients
Leftover grilled chicken, about 1 cup for appetizer, 2 cups for a meal
12 ounces tortilla chips
1 16-ounce can of black beans, rinsed and drained
1 cup Queso fresco cheese, crumbled or shredded Monterey Jack
Juice of two limes plus zest
Juice of one lemon plus zest
3 Roma tomatoes, chopped
2 gloves garlic, minced
1 jalapeno, roasted and skinned
1 red bell pepper, diced
1/4 of a red onion, diced
1 tablespoon olive oil
1 teaspoon chili powder
Salt and pepper
1/2 cup chopped cilantro
1/2 cup sour cream
Jalapeno slices

Directions

Prepare salsa by combining juice of lemon and limes, tomatoes, garlic, jalapeno, red bell pepper, onion, olive oil, and chili powder. Salt and pepper to taste. Let flavors blend in the refrigerator at least 30 minutes.

To build the nachos, spread tortilla chips on baking pan. Layer the grilled chicken, then zest, black beans, and cheese over chips. Bake in a 400ºF oven just until cheese melts, about 5 minutes. Top with salsa, cilantro, sour cream and jalapeno slices and serve immediately.

Rosemary Citrus Grilled Turkey Breast with Mango Salsa

This recipe calls for orange, lime, lemon and grapefruit juices to give a unique flavor to the turkey, sweet, juicy, perfect for the summer months. You have to prepare in advance because it takes 12 to 18 hours to marinate.

Serves 6

Ingredients
1 turkey breast of 31/2 to 4 pounds, bone-in

Marinade Ingredients
1/4 cup freshly squeezed orange juice
1/4 cup freshly squeezed lime juice
1/4 cup fresh lemon juice
1/4 cup freshly squeezed grapefruit juice
1/4 cup brown sugar
2 cloves garlic
1 tablespoon of fresh rosemary, chopped
1 teaspoon grated fresh ginger
1 teaspoon kosher salt
1/2 teaspoon black pepper
1/2 cup soya sauce
1 tablespoon Worcestershire sauce

Mango Salsa ingredients
1 tablespoon olive oil
2 tablespoons freshly squeezed lime juice
1 garlic clove, minced

2 mangos, peeled and cubed
1 heirloom tomato, cubed
3 green onions, white and light green parts minced
½ green bell pepper, cubed
2 tablespoons raw honey
1 tablespoon fresh cilantro, chopped
1-2 pinches of crushed chilies to taste
Sea salt & fresh ground pepper to taste

Directions
Stir all ingredients from the marinade together in a mixing bowl and mix well. Reserve 1/2 cup of the marinade aside in the refrigerator. Place the turkey breast in an extra-large plastic bag such as zip lock, add remaining marinade and seal tightly. Let it rest in the refrigerator for at least 12 hours and up to 18 hours.

Remove the turkey breast from the bag and let rest for 30 minutes before cooking.

Insert a meat thermometer in the turkey meat where it is the thickest, without touching any bones, set to it 170°F. Start the BBQ at low temperature of 300°F. When BBQ is ready, place the turkey in the middle of the grill, close lid and grill turkey for 1h½-2h00, checking the thermometer regularly.

In the meantime, prepare mango salsa, place all ingredients in a mixing bowl and stir well. Season with salt and pepper to taste. Cover with plastic wrap and let rest at room temperature for 15-20 minutes before serving.

After 1h15, brush the turkey with the reserved marinade. After it has reached an internal temperature of 170°F on the thermometer, remove the turkey from the BBQ and place on a cutting board. Let it rest 10 to 15 minutes before slicing. Serve with the mango-cranberry salsa.

Sweet Barbecue Pulled Chicken Sliders

These sliders are juicy and can be served open-face. Grill extra chicken next time you fire up the grill and make these later in the week for a quick delicious dinner. Serve coleslaw or beans with the sliders.

Serves 4–6

Ingredients
4 boneless chicken breasts
1 package Hawaiian-style rolls
1 16-ounce can crushed pineapple with juice
1/2 cup All-Purpose Cider BBQ Sauce
1/4 cup soy sauce
1/4 cup mirin (rice vinegar)
2 scallions, diced
Olive oil
Salt
Pepper

Directions
Preheat grill to medium-high.

Rub chicken breasts with salt, pepper and olive oil. When grill is hot, grill chicken breasts 10–12 minutes each side. Remove from heat and allow to cool. Shred chicken with two forks and place in a mixing bowl. Combine the pineapple, juice, BBQ sauce, soy sauce, mirin and mix together. Add the shredded chicken and stir to coat well.

Slice rolls and toast lightly. Spoon chicken mixture onto rolls and top with diced scallions.

Fish and Seafood

Seafood-Stuffed Grilled Green Chilies

Texas' proximity to the Gulf of Mexico means plenty of fresh seafood. Here, the fresh shrimp are tucked into another Texas staple, the green chili. This recipe is easily doubled or tripled for large gatherings and can be cooked on the grill with other food.

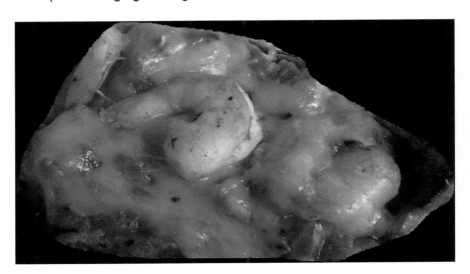

Serves 4

Ingredients
4 fresh chilies, flame-roasted and peeled
1/2 pound fresh shrimp, peeled, deveined and roughly chopped
1 tablespoon olive oil
1 tablespoon butter
1/4 cup chopped red onion
1/4 cup chopped red tomatoes
2 green onions, sliced
1/2 cup chopped red bell pepper
1/2 teaspoon chili powder
2 tablespoons white wine
1 egg, beaten
1 cup shredded Monterey Jack cheese
Salt and freshly ground pepper

Directions

Heat the oil and butter in a large skillet on medium-high heat. Add the onion, cook 2–3 minutes, then, add shrimp, tomatoes, green onions, bell pepper, chili powder and wine. Cook until shrimp are opaque, about 3 minutes. Remove from heat and set aside to cool.

When cool, stir in egg and cheese. Salt and pepper to taste.

Preheat grill.

Cut a slit down each chili and remove seeds. Spoon about 1/2 cup of shrimp mixture into the chilies. Close up and place in an oiled cast iron skillet. Cover and seal with foil. Place on hot grill and cook about 8–12 minutes.

Bronzed Catch of the Day

The trend of "blackening" fish has fallen out of favor due to its carcinogenic properties. This method provides some of the salty, spicy flavor in a healthier way. The bronzer recipe is good on many fishes, and shrimps.

Serves 4

Ingredients
1 1/2 pounds white fish such as cod, tilapia or catfish. Fish fillets should be about ½ inch thick to insure even cooking.
3 ounces of unsalted butter

For the Bronzer
1 tablespoon sea salt
1 1/2 teaspoon garlic powder
1 1/2 teaspoon onion powder
1 1/2 teaspoon high-quality paprika
1 teaspoon red pepper flakes
2 teaspoons black pepper
1 teaspoon white pepper
1 teaspoon ground cumin
1 teaspoon ground oregano
1 1/2 teaspoons dried basil
1 1/2 teaspoons dried thyme

Directions

Rinse and pat fish fillets dry. Combine all bronzing ingredients into a bowl and mix well. Sprinkle about 1 to 1 1/2 tablespoons of the bronzer on the fish fillets.

Preheat grill to medium-high heat.

Heat the butter in a large cast iron skillet until the butter just begins to brown. Place the fish fillets in the pan. Cook about 2 1/2 minutes on each side, being careful to not overcook. Remove from heat and serve immediately.

Grilled Red Snapper with Grilled Vegetables

Gulf coast red snapper have a limited fishing season, usually June or July. If you can get the fresh fish, it is fantastic. Simple grilled vegetables are a perfect accompaniment and a beautiful presentation.

Serves 4

Ingredients
4 6–8 ounce red snapper fillets
1/4 cup olive oil, approximately
1 lemon, quartered
2 tablespoons lemon juice
Salt and freshly ground pepper
1 zucchini, diced
2 yellow bell peppers, sliced
2 red bell peppers, sliced
1 red onion, diced
2 cloves garlic, sliced
1/2 cup Kalamata olives, pitted
1 teaspoon fresh oregano
2 tablespoons capers
Fresh flat leave parsley for garnish

Directions
Preheat grill to a medium temperature.

Wash and dry fish fillets. Lightly brush with olive oil then apply salt, pepper, and lemon juice. Let rest.

Meanwhile, cut all vegetables. Drizzle with remaining olive oil and toss to coat.

Place fish on the heated grill and the vegetables in a cast iron pan directly on the grill. Fish will take about 4–6 minutes each side. Vegetables should be crisp-tender when removed from heat. To serve, place grilled vegetables on a large platter. Sprinkle oregano, capers and basil over them. Remove fish from grill and place on platter over vegetables. Serve with lemon quarters.

Spiced BBQ Salmon

Salmon is one of the best fish you can grill. This recipe's rich flavors will shine through and make you want to do this recipe over and over again.

Serves 6

Ingredients
6 salmon steaks
All-Purpose Chicken & Fish Marinade
1 teaspoon chili powder
1/4 teaspoon cumin

Directions
Wash and dry the salmon steaks. Place steaks on a dish and brush each side with about 1 tablespoon each of the All-Purpose Chicken & Fish Marinade. Let rest 20–30 minutes while you preheat the grill to 325°F.

When grill is hot, sprinkle the chili powder and cumin over each side of the salmon steaks. Place on the grill and cook 4–6 minutes each side until it begins to flake.

Grilled Skewered Shrimp

The skewered shrimp can be served as an appetizer or on a bed of rice for a meal. They cook quickly, so don't leave them unattended or they will dry out and become rubbery.

Serves 6–8

Ingredients
2 pounds raw medium shrimp, peeled and deveined
1/2 cup butter, melted
1/4 cup olive oil
1/2 cup white wine like Chardonnay or Pinot Grigio
3 cloves garlic, minced
1 lemon, juiced
Sea salt and freshly ground pepper

3 tablespoons cilantro, chopped
3 tablespoons basil, chopped
Skewers

Directions

If using wooden skewers, soak in water while shrimp marinate. Preheat grill.

Combine butter, olive oil, wine, garlic, lemon juice, salt and pepper in mixing bowl. Mix well; add shrimp, mixing to coat. Cover and place in refrigerator up to 30 minutes.

Push skewer through shrimp in two places so the shrimp form a "c." (Hint: this keeps them from turning on the grill). Place shrimp skewers on hot grill, turning after 3 minutes. Cook an additional 2–3 minutes just until done. Remove from heat and place on serving platter. Sprinkle with cilantro, basil and additional salt and pepper to taste.

Smoky Crab Cakes

Crab cakes are far too delicate to consider putting on the grill. However, place a cast iron skillet on the grill and the cakes will do nicely. A bit of liquid smoke creates the desired smoky flavor.

Serves 6

Ingredients
1 pound jumbo lump crab meat
1/2 to 3/4 cup breadcrumbs
1/4 cup onion, 1/4 inch dice
1/2 cup celery, 1/4 inch dice
1/2 cup red bell pepper, 1/4 inch dice
1/2 cup green bell pepper, 1/4 inch dice
1 egg, beaten
1 tablespoon lemon juice
1/2 teaspoon liquid smoke
1 teaspoon Worcestershire sauce
1/2 teaspoon cayenne pepper
1/8 teaspoon black pepper
3 tablespoons fresh parsley, chopped
2–3 tablespoons butter

Directions

Clean crab meat, removing any bits of shell and set aside. Measure breadcrumbs and set aside.

In a large mixing bowl combine the onion, celery, bell peppers and stir. Add the beaten egg, lemon juice, liquid smoke, Worcestershire sauce, cayenne pepper, black pepper, and parsley and mix.

Add the crab mix and mix gently. Next, add 1/2 cup breadcrumbs. The mixture should hold together without being too wet. If needed, add the additional breadcrumbs. Divide mixture into 6 sections. Form each patty by packing together moderately firmly.

Heat butter in large skillet over medium heat. In two batches, fry patties until golden brown, turning once. Remove and keep warm in foil in oven until ready to serve. Serve your favorite with spicy red sauce.

Starters & Sides

Texas Fries

There is evidence that "French fries" may actually have been invented by a Texan who was from Paris, TX. The misnomer comes from where he lived. These are big, hearty wedges with a bit of lively seasoning.

Serves 4–6

Ingredients
4 russet baking potatoes, well washed
1 tablespoon chili powder
1/4 teaspoon cayenne
1/4 teaspoon ground cumin
1/2 teaspoon sugar
3 tablespoons olive oil
Salt and fresh ground pepper to taste

Directions

Bake the potatoes until done. (Microwaving is fine and saves time). When cool enough to handle, slice the potatoes in 6 pieces lengthwise.

Combine chili powder, cayenne, cumin, sugar, and olive oil in a small bowl and mix well. Generously salt and pepper the potato wedges. Spread the prepared olive oil mixture onto the potato wedge. Just before serving, place potatoes on hot grill to finish.

Grilled Squash Southwestern Casserole

Squash Casserole is a Texas tradition. Grilling the vegetables heightens the flavor and reduces the water content so the casserole is not too mushy after baking.

Ingredients
3 yellow (summer) squash, sliced
3 zucchini, sliced
1 medium onion, peeled
4 Anaheim green chilies
1 jalapeno chili, optional
3 cloves garlic, minced
1/2 cup grated cheddar cheese
1/2 cup grated Monterey Jack cheese
1/2 cup sour cream
1/2 cup grated parmesan cheese
1 cup crushed butter crackers
2 tablespoons butter, room temperature
Olive oil
Salt and freshly ground pepper

Directions

Char the chilies over flame until blackened on all sides. Immediately place chilis in plastic bag and set aside.

Rub olive oil on the sliced yellow squash, zucchini, and onion; salt and pepper. Place the vegetables on the grill, until softened and charred, about 3–4 minutes each side. Remove from heat.

Peel the blackened skin off the cooled chili; seed and stem. Dice.

Combine garlic, cheddar cheese, Monterey Jack cheese, and sour cream. Add the cooked squash, onion and chilies and mix gently. Adjust salt and pepper to taste. Butter a squared 9 inch casserole dish. Place squash mixture into dish. Dot the top of the mixture with the butter and sprinkle with grated parmesan and crushed butter crackers. Bake uncovered, in a 325°F oven, about 15 minutes until top is golden brown.

Spicy Grilled Corn-on-the-Cob

There is no reason the vegetables (OK, starch) can't be done on the grill along with the meat. This recipe calls for cilantro but other herbs like oregano and basil are also delicious. Try your favorite.

Serves 6

Ingredients
6 ears of corn, in husk
1/4 cup sea salt
2 tablespoons paprika
1/2 teaspoons black pepper
1 small clove garlic
3/4 cup fresh cilantro, packed
1 lime
Chives for garnish

Directions
Prepare the corn by peeling back the husks and removing the silks. Soak the corn, with husks, in water about 30 minutes prior to grilling.

Combine the salt, paprika, black pepper, garlic and cilantro in a food processor. Pulse until cilantro is well incorporated. Set aside.

After soaking, drain and rub the corn with lime juice. Grill on hot grill, with husks peeled back, about 8–10 minutes, turning until all sides have charred. Remove from grill. Apply the reserved spice mixture to the corncobs. Close up husks. Return to grill until just warm and serve with chives snippets and butter.

Warm German Potato Salad

The Texas Hill Country has a large population of German, Czech and other European immigrants. This potato salad honors them for making something else even better with bacon.

Serves 6

Ingredients
4 pounds of red potatoes, peeled and sliced 1/4 inch thick
1 pound of bacon, cut into 1 inch pieces
1 red onion, sliced
1 tablespoon flour
1 tablespoon sugar
2 teaspoons mustard powder
About 1 teaspoon each of salt and pepper, or to taste
1/3 cup red wine vinegar
2/3 cup water
1 green onion, diced
Fresh parsley

Directions

Set a pot of water to boil. Place sliced potatoes in boiling water; cook about 12 minutes or until just tender. Remove from pot so they do not overcook and place in large baking pan.

Meanwhile, cook bacon until slightly crisp and remove from pan to drain.

Reserve the drippings and cook the onions in the drippings until well browned and caramelized. In the same pan, add the flour, sugar, mustard powder, salt, and pepper. Mix, then add the vinegar and water and stir until thickened.
Remove from heat and add the bacon. Pour entire mixture over the potatoes and stir gently to coat.

The dish can be served immediately or re-warmed in the oven (covered). Sprinkle with fresh parsley.

Mustard Potato Salad (Chilled)

Various regions of the United States have their version of this classic. This Texan version has peppers and a carrot for a little splash of color and flavor.

Serves 6

Ingredients
1 pound yellow or gold potatoes, cubed
1/4 cup onion, finely chopped (1/4 inch dice)
1/2 cup green bell pepper, finely chopped
1/4 cup celery, finely chopped
1 carrot, finely chopped
¼ cup red onions, chopped
Fresh cilantro (or parsley), chopped
Paprika

Dressing
2 teaspoons whole-grain mustard
2 teaspoons yellow mustard
2 tablespoons mayonnaise
1/4 cup apple cider vinegar
2 teaspoons sugar

1 teaspoons salt
Fresh ground pepper to taste

Directions
Cook diced potatoes in boiling water until fork tender, about 12–14 minutes. Do not overcook. Drain and allow to cool. Combine with next 6 ingredients in a large mixing bowl.

Combine all dressing ingredients in a bowl and mix until well blended. Pour over potato mixture and stir to blend. Chill until serving and sprinkle with paprica.

Smokin' Hot BBQ Beans

No Texas barbecue is complete without plenty of beans. This easy version uses canned beans, but the additional ingredients make them special.

Serves 6–8

Ingredients
2 cans baked beans, 15 ounces each
1 can black beans, 15 ounces, drained
1 cup purchased barbecue sauce
3 shallots, diced
1 red bell pepper, seeded and diced
2 cloves garlic, minced
1/2 pound bacon, diced, cooked, and drained
1 poblano pepper, seeded and diced
1 jalapeno pepper, seeded and diced
1 granny smith apple, cored, peeled and finely diced
1/4 cup dark brown sugar
1/4 cup Dijon mustard
1 teaspoon liquid smoke
Salt and freshly ground pepper

Directions

Combine all ingredients into a large pot. Cook covered, over very low heat, stirring occasionally and adjusting seasoning to taste. Beans should be heated 30–45 minutes to blend flavors well.

Grilled Pineapple Coleslaw

Sweet, spicy, cool and refreshing. A lighter side dish nicely paired with a grilled or smoked meat.

Serves 4–6

Ingredients
1 large ripe pineapple, peeled, cored and sliced into 1/2 inch slices, reserve juice
1 cabbage, about 1.5 pounds, cored
1 carrot, peeled
1 green onion, finely diced
1 or 2 jalapenos, finely diced
1 1/2 cups plain yogurt
1/2 cup mayonnaise
3 tablespoons Dijon mustard
1 tablespoon sugar (optional)
2 tablespoons fresh lime juice
Salt and freshly ground pepper
Olive oil

Directions

Rub pineapple slices with olive oil on both sides. Place on hot grill, turning once, until golden. Cool, then, cut into bite-size chunks.

Shred the cabbage and carrot in a food processor. Toss into a large mixing bowl with green onions and jalapenos. In a small bowl, combine yogurt, mayonnaise, Dijon, sugar and lime juice. Pour over cabbage and carrots, add pineapple, with any juice, and mix gently until well coated. Season with salt and pepper.

Chill several hours until ready to serve. Goes well with any grilled meats.

Texas Deviled Eggs

These are usually the first appetizer to run out on any table. People love them but seem to forget they do until they see them. The Texas spin puts a load of appetizing color on them.

Makes 24 eggs

Ingredients
12 eggs, hard-boiled
1/4 cup mayonnaise
1 tablespoon pickle relish
1 tablespoon yellow mustard
1 tablespoon hot sauce (I like to use Sriracha sauce)
1–2 teaspoons Worcestershire sauce
Salt and freshly ground pepper

For Garnish
2 tablespoons chives, very finely minced
2 tablespoons red bell pepper, very finely minced
Paprika

Directions

While eggs are boiling, prepare garnish. Dice chives and red pepper very finely and keep each separate. Peel shell off of the cooled eggs. Slice eggs in half and remove yolks.

Combine yolks in mixing bowl with mayonnaise, relish, mustard, Sriracha sauce and Worcestershire sauce. Add salt and pepper to taste.

Fill each of the sliced eggs with about a tablespoon of the yolk mixture until all is used. Garnish each egg with a sprinkle of red bell pepper, chives and paprika.

Chill until serving time.

Cucumber Salad

Cucumber salad is quite simple to make but has a complex, refreshing taste. It's perfect with spicy, hot foods.

Serves 4

Ingredients

2 cucumbers
1/2 of a small red onion
1 small chili pepper (jalapeno or red chili)
1 large clove garlic
2 tablespoons sugar
2 tablespoons rice vinegar
1/2 water, warmed

Directions
Slice cucumbers, onion, chili and garlic very thinly. A mandolin works best to get the vegetables sliced very thin. Arrange the vegetables on the serving platter.

Mix sugar, rice vinegar and warm water in a small dish until sugar dissolves. Pour over vegetables and chill until serving time.

Sweet Endings

Texas Pecan Pie

Pecans are a major crop in Texas and they are used in a lot of great recipes. One of the best is a classic pecan pie. Simple and delicious throughout the year.

Serves 6-8

Ingredients
Crust (makes 1)
1 cup all-purpose flour
6 tablespoons butter, cold
2 tablespoons shortening
1/4 cup ice water
1/4 teaspoon salt

Filling
1/3 cup butter
1/2 cup white sugar
1 cup light corn syrup
1 tablespoon vanilla extract
4 eggs, slightly beaten
1 teaspoon salt
2 cups pecan halves

Directions
Preheat oven to 350ºF.

To form the crust, dissolve the salt in the water and set aside. Combine flour and shortening, blending until crumbles are about the size of peas. Add the salted water slowly; continue mixing until dough forms a smooth ball. Roll dough out on lightly floured surface until about 1/8 inch thick. Place in 10-inch pie pan.

Melt the butter and remove from heat. Combine with white sugar, corn syrup, vanilla, eggs, and salt. Pour into prepared crust. Spread pecan halves on top.

Bake on cookie sheet in 350ºF degree oven for 45–50 minutes or until set. (A toothpick will come out clean when inserted.)

Cool completely before cutting into 6 or 8 servings.

Strawberry Shortcakes

Several areas of Texas grow strawberries and when they are at their ripest, people rush to get their fill. The cheesy cakes in this recipe work nicely with all berries so feel free to substitute with any of your favorites.

Makes 6 large servings

Ingredients
1 pint fresh strawberries, washed, stemmed, and sliced (any berries may be used)
1 1/2 cups all-purpose flour
2 teaspoons baking powder
1 teaspoon cinnamon
1/2 teaspoon salt
1/2 teaspoon baking soda
2 tablespoons cold unsalted butter, diced
1 1/2 cups shredded Monterey Jack cheese
1 cup sour cream
Whipping cream

Directions
Preheat oven to 425°F.

Sift together flour, baking powder, cinnamon, salt and soda into a mixing bowl. Add the butter and blend with a pastry tool until mixture forms coarse crumbs, about the size of peas. Stir in the cheese, then add sour cream. Stir until the mixture forms a soft dough.

Turn out the dough on a lightly floured surface and knead 6 times. Roll the dough out until 1/2 inch thick. Cut with a 3 1/3 inch round cutter. Bake on ungreased baking sheet 15–17 minutes until golden brown. Cool on wire rack.

To assemble, cut cakes in half, add plenty of sliced strawberries, cover with the other cake's half. Arrange some more strawberry slices. Garnish with whipped cream and enjoy.

Peach Ice Cream

Vanilla is still the most popular ice cream flavor in the United States. Perhaps it's because it is so versatile, especially when you mix in other flavors. Roasting the peaches enhances the flavor.

Makes about a quart.

Ingredients
6 medium peaches, roasted
2 cups half and half
1 cup whipping cream
1/2 cup sugar
1/8 teaspoon cinnamon
1/2 peach preserves
1 whole vanilla bean, split and scraped out
Salt
Brown sugar

Directions
Peaches – Preheat oven to 400ºF.

Pit and halve the peaches and place on baking sheet, cut side down. Sprinkle with about 2 tablespoons of brown sugar. Roast for about 30 minutes. Let cool and remove the skins. Chop into 1 inch pieces. Retain juices with peaches and store in refrigerator.

Ice Cream – Combine all ingredients except peaches in a saucepan. Bring the mixture to 170ºF over medium heat (barely simmering), stirring occasionally. Remove from heat and strain the mixture into a lidded container. Cool the mixture in the refrigerator overnight.

Freeze mixture in the ice cream machine according to manufacturer's instructions. At the halfway point, stir in reserved peaches and juices. Finish churning in machine. When complete, spoon into lidded container and freeze at least 2 hours before serving.

Brownie Bites

This is an easy version using your favorite boxed brownie mix. The fun comes with the variety of decorative toppings that you finish them with. I chose sweet coconut and colored sugar in this recipe but you can your imagination and use others.

Makes 24 bites.

Ingredients
1 box of 9 x 13 brownie mix (and the ingredients on the box)
½ cup icing sugar
½ cup fine sweetened coconut flakes
1 cup colored refined sugar
Wax paper

Directions
Prepare the pan and bake the brownies according to package directions.

Let cool slightly. While still warm, cut brownies into 24 pieces. Quickly roll up each cut brownie into a ball. Place icing sugar and coconut flakes in a large shallow dish. In another similar dish, place colored sugar. Roll half of the brownie balls into icing sugar mixed with sweetened coconut, roll the other half in colored sugar. Place all brownies on wax paper-lined cookie sheet and chill to set, at least 1 hour before serving.

Conclusion

We hope you enjoy the Texas BBQ recipes included here. It's a sampler of techniques and local ingredients that represent BBQ throughout the state. Experienced or novice cooks can impress their friends and family at the next outdoor get-together.

Happy BBQing!

Made in the USA
Lexington, KY
10 June 2014